Insects

Insects

Published by
Heron Books, Inc.
20950 SW Rock Creek Road
Sheridan, OR 97378

heronbooks.com

Special thanks to all the teachers and students who
provided feedback instrumental to this edition.

Third Edition © 1978, 2022 Heron Books.
All Rights Reserved

ISBN: 978-0-89-739282-2

Printed in the USA

30 October 2022

LEARNING
at the
SPEED
of *You*

At Heron Books, we think learning should be engaging and fun. It should be hands-on and allow students to move at their own pace.

To facilitate this we have created a learning guide that will help any student progress through this book, chapter by chapter, with confidence and interest.

Get learning guides at
heronbooks.com/learningguides.

For teacher resources,
such as a final exam, email
teacherresources@heronbooks.com.

We would love to hear from you!
Email us at *feedback@heronbooks.com.*

IN THIS BOOK

Chapter 1

How Are Insects Alike?

Chapter 1

How Are Insects Alike?

So aren't all insects just bugs? Well, there are some animals you might think of as bugs that are not actually insects. For example, a spider is not an insect! But insects and spiders are alike in some ways.

A group of animals that is alike in some important ways is called a **class**. There is a class of animals that don't have bones inside their bodies. Instead of bones inside, they have hard coverings outside their bodies. The name of this class of animals is **invertebrate** (in VER tuh brit). And this class includes insects, spiders, centipedes, and crabs!

spider

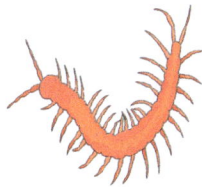
centipede

crab

So now we know one way insects are similar to spiders and centipedes—they are invertebrates.

But what is it that makes an insect an *insect?*

INSECTS HAVE SIX LEGS.

INSECTS HAVE TWO FEELERS ON THEIR HEADS.

Insects can feel things and smell things with their feelers.

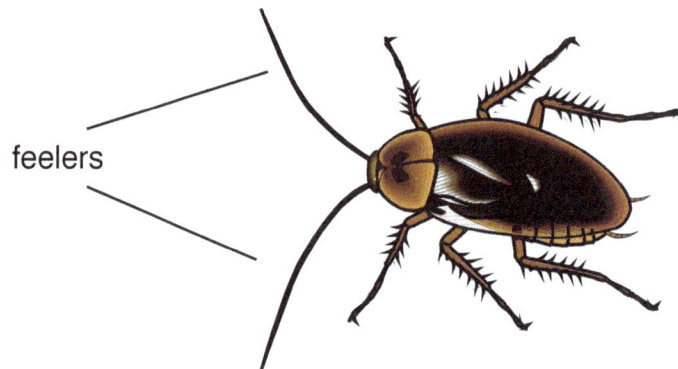

feelers

INSECTS HAVE THREE MAIN BODY PARTS.

1. The head.

The head has the eyes, mouth, brain and feelers.

2.   The thorax.

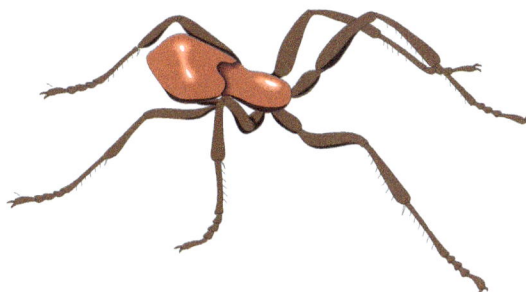

The thorax has the legs, and wings if there are any. Most of the insects' muscles are in the thorax.

3.   The abdomen.

The abdomen of an insect has the parts that breathe air and digest food. It is made up of several sections like rings.

ALMOST ALL INSECTS HATCH FROM EGGS.

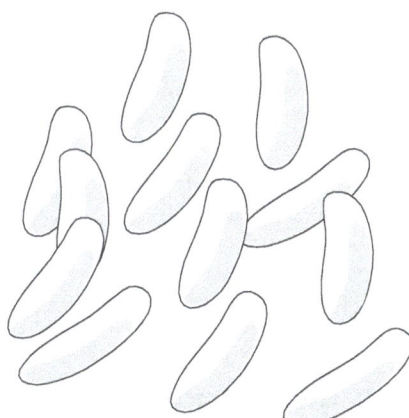

SO WHAT ABOUT SPIDERS?

So now that you know what makes an insect an insect, you can tell why spiders are not insects.

Spiders have eight legs, not six.

Spiders have no feelers.

There are only two main parts to their bodies, not three, because the head and thorax are not separated.

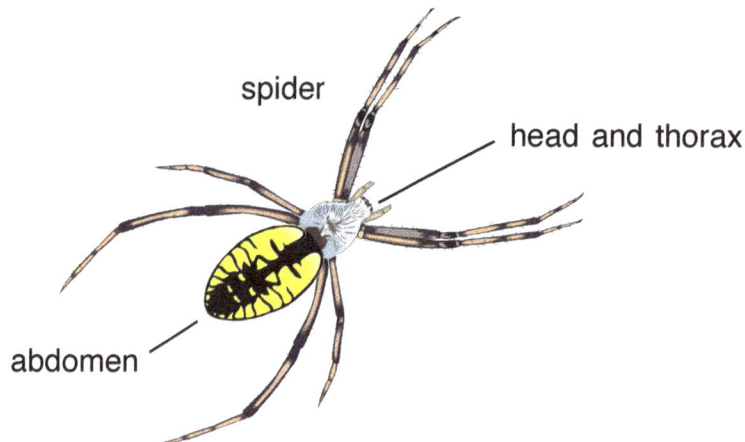

spider

head and thorax

abdomen

HOW ARE INSECTS ALIKE?

They have six legs.

They have two feelers on their heads.

They have three main body parts.

Almost all hatch from eggs.

LET'S DO THIS!
How Insects Are Alike

For this activity you will need

- an insect and spider, preserved or found
- access to the internet or picture books or magazines of insects

Steps

INSECTS HAVE SIX LEGS

1. Look at a real insect (preserved or one you find). Count the legs.

2. Look at pictures of other insects online or in a book or magazine. Count the legs.

INSECTS HAVE TWO FEELERS ON THEIR HEADS

3. Look at the insect and find the feelers.

4. Look at pictures of other insects and find the feelers.

INSECTS HAVE THREE MAIN BODY PARTS

5. Look at the real insect. Find the head, the thorax and the abdomen.

6. Look at pictures of other insects and find all those parts.

7. What part are the feelers attached to?

8. What part are the legs (and any wings) attached to?

ALMOST ALL INSECTS HATCH FROM EGGS.

9. Look at pictures of insect eggs online or in a book or magazine.

COMPARE OTHER BUGS

10. Look at a spider (preserved or one you find). List what you see that can tell you it is not an insect.

11. Look at pictures of a centipede. List what you see that can tell you it is not an insect.

Chapter 2

The Life of an Insect

The Life of an Insect

When insects are grown up, they **mate**. This means that a male and a female get together so they can make baby insects. The female insect then lays her eggs. Insects lay their eggs in safe places such as on trees, on plants or in the ground. Some insects may lay thousands of eggs!

After a time of a few days up to a month in the egg, the baby insect hatches out of the egg.

Baby insects do not follow the rules about how adult insects look. For instance, instead of six legs, baby insects may have no legs at all, or many legs. They often look more like worms than like the adult insects they will become.

As baby insects grow up their bodies don't just get bigger. They also change how they look. In fact, they go through a *big* change. This big change is called **metamorphosis** (met-ah-MORE-fo-sis), which means "changing to a different shape."

METAMORPHOSIS OF A BUTTERFLY

A baby butterfly is a caterpillar.

When the caterpillar is older, it hangs on a twig and covers itself up. Inside the cover it changes very slowly. This change is the metamorphosis.

After a while, the caterpillar has changed and a butterfly crawls out of the covering that the caterpillar went into.

COMPLETE METAMORPHOSIS

Many kinds of insects change in four parts. This kind of change is called **complete metamorphosis**. A butterfly is one kind of insect that does complete metamorphosis by changing four times.

PART ONE—EGG

The first part of a butterfly's life is the egg.

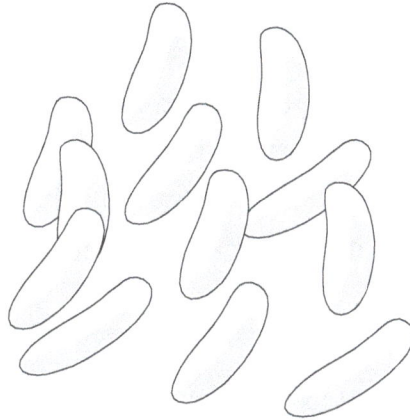

PART TWO—LARVA

When a butterfly hatches from its egg, it is a caterpillar. Another word for an insect in this part of its life is **larva**.

When you are talking about more than one larva, you say larvae (LAR-vee).

Larvae eat leaves and sometimes dead plants and animals. They grow very fast and eat more than adult insects do.

Before we talk more about how insects grow, there is another interesting thing to learn about. The hard coverings insects have outside their bodies cannot stretch very much because they have to be tough to protect them.

To grow bigger, they have to shed their old covering. First they grow a new soft covering inside the old hard one. Then they shed the old one by crawling out of it. Because the new covering is still soft, they can get bigger by stretching it. Then the new covering hardens up, and the insect can't grow much until they shed that covering. When an insect sheds its old covering, it is called **molting**.

Larvae have fairly soft coverings that can stretch quite a bit. But they can't always stretch enough, so larvae usually molt several times during this part of their lives, getting bigger each time.

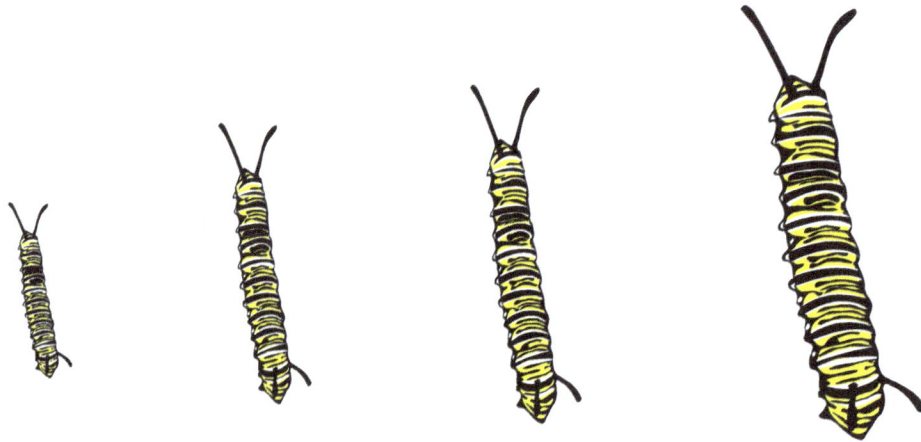

PART THREE—PUPA

When the larva has grown about as much as it can, it is ready for the big change. It attaches itself to something like a twig or a leaf, and sheds its skin. What is underneath is a case called a **cocoon** that covers and protects the larva.

This is the third part of complete metamorphosis. While the insect is in this part of its life, it is called a **pupa** (PEW-puh). The plural of pupa is pupae (PEW-pee).

The pupa does not move or eat for many days, but inside the cocoon, the body of the insect is changing again.

PART FOUR—ADULT

Finally, what comes out of the cocoon is the adult insect—in this case the butterfly! The adult is the last part of complete metamorphosis.

Do you see now why this is called a metamorphosis? The insect looks completely different in each of these parts of its life!

INCOMPLETE METAMORPHOSIS

Some kinds of insects grow up in three parts. This is called *incomplete* metamorphosis. The grasshopper is a good example of this kind of metamorphosis. It changes three times.

PART ONE—EGG

The first part of a grasshopper's life is the egg.

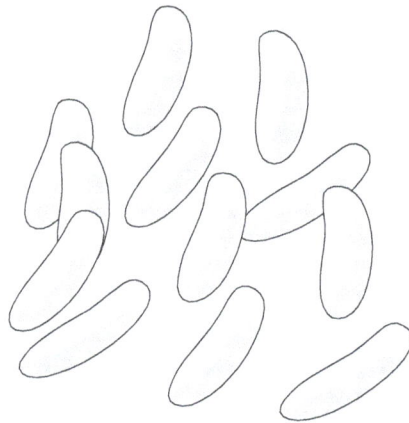

PART TWO—NYMPH

When a grasshopper hatches from its egg, it is called a **nymph** (nimf). The nymphs look like small grasshoppers, they just don't have full-size wings.

The nymphs of some insects don't look so much like the adults. Dragonfly nymphs, for example, have much fatter bodies than the adults. They don't have wings, and live under water.

As a nymph grows, it molts and sheds its covering several times. A nymph may keep molting and growing for several months.

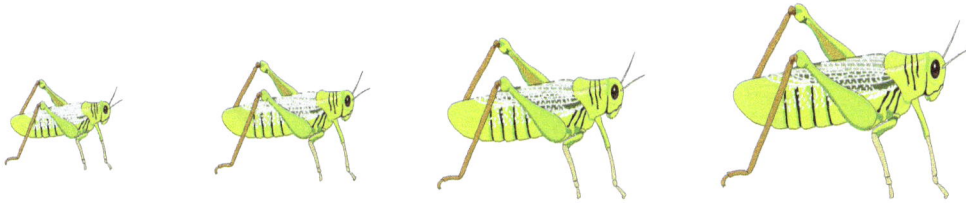

PART THREE—ADULT

The third and last part of a grasshopper's life is adult. It molts one last time and comes out of its old skin in adult form, complete with full size wings. The adult grasshopper is fully grown.

THE LIFE OF AN INSECT

So now you know how insects live their lives.

Complete metamorphosis: egg, larva, pupa, adult.

Incomplete metamorphosis: egg, nymph, adult.

LET'S DO THIS!
The Life of an Insect

For this activity you will need

- drawing materials
- modeling clay

Steps

PART ONE

1. Make a drawing of an insect molting.

2. Show it to another person, and explain how an insect grows.

3. Use clay to make a model of the four parts of an insect's complete metamorphosis.

4. When you're done, show it to another person, and explain what a complete metamorphosis is.

PART TWO

5. Use clay to make a model of the three parts of an insect's incomplete metamorphosis.

6. When you're done, show it to another person, and explain what an incomplete metamorphosis is.

Chapter 3

Social Insects

Chapter 3

Social Insects

Social means getting along well with others. **Social insects** are insects which live and work together in groups. In a group of social insects each insect works for the survival of the group, not just itself.

Ants, honeybees, certain wasps and termites are social insects. (Termites are kind of like ants, but they live mostly in dead wood.)

ant   termite   bee   wasp

A **colony** is a group of people or animals living together. In a colony of social insects there are three kinds of insects: the queens, the males (also called drones) and the workers.

worker   queen   drone

These three kinds of insects work together to help the group live. Each kind has a job to help the group.

QUEEN

The job of the queen is to lay eggs. She is actually the mother of all the other insects in her colony. Usually you can recognize a queen because she has a big abdomen where she carries her eggs.

DRONES

The drones are bigger than most other members of the colony. Drones have only one job, and that is to mate with a queen to fertilize her eggs. **Fertilize** means to make the eggs ready to grow and hatch.

After just one mating, a queen ant or bee will be able to make fertile eggs for the rest of her life. So drone bees or ants often die after mating. If they do not die, the drones usually stay in the nest and are fed by the workers. But they do no work themselves, so if food is scarce, they do not get anything to eat.

A drone termite, on the other hand, becomes a "king" when he mates with a queen, and he will stay with her for life, helping her to build a nest and mating with her again and again.

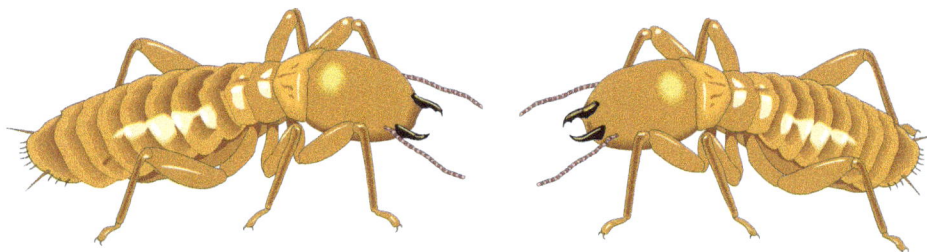

queen   king

WORKERS

The workers are female, like the queen, but the workers are small and usually do not lay any eggs. The workers have many jobs. They take care of the queen, the males, the eggs, the larvae and the pupae. They clean the nest, and gather food.

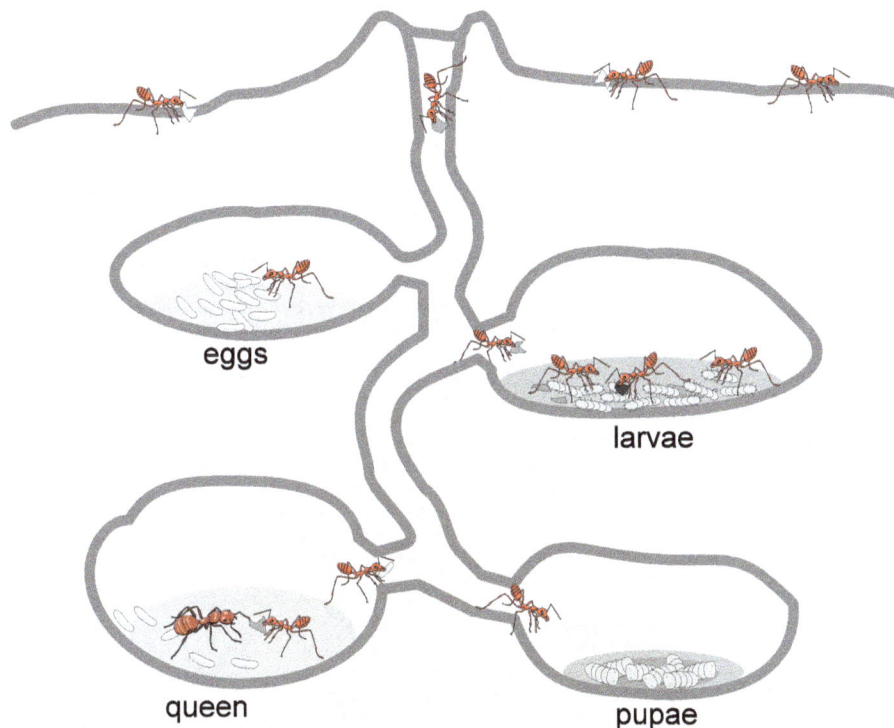

eggs

larvae

queen

pupae

Some workers build the nests or hives for the colony to live and grow in.

wasp nest

In a colony of ants or termites, some of the workers may be "soldiers." They have the job of defending the colony from attack by enemies. These soldiers are usually bigger and stronger than regular workers.

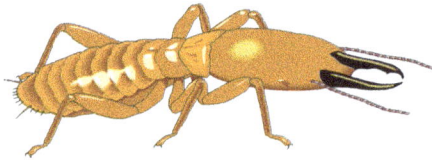

soldier termite   soldier ant

In a colony of bees, some of the worker bees make honey and store it in the many holes of the honeycomb.

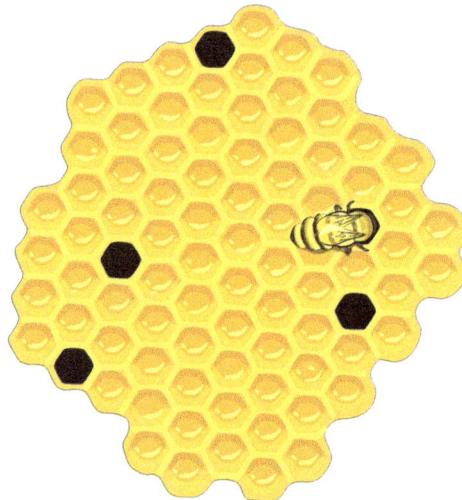

honeycomb

The honeycomb itself is made by other worker bees.

In a bee colony, workers can feed a female larva a special food they make called *royal jelly*. This makes that larva grow big and become a queen. Female larvae that are not fed royal jelly all grow into more workers.

When there are a lot of workers and plenty of food is brought into the nest, then more royal jelly is made and more larvae can grow into queens.

When the new queens grow up, they mate, and then fly away from their colony to start a new one. Some of the bees from the old colony may go with a new queen, or she may start a new nest by herself.

As soon as the new nest is made, the queen starts to lay eggs. When the new eggs hatch and grow to be adult workers, they start to take care of the queen and help build the new colony.

You can see why these are called social insects. They work together by doing their jobs and making their groups strong and able to continue living.

LET'S DO THIS!
Social Insects

For this activity you will need

- access to internet
- drawing materials or modeling clay

Steps

1. Have an adult help you find a video of the inside of a bee hive showing eggs, larvae, and queen. Also find a picture of the inside of a termite mound.

2. Draw or use clay to show a social insect colony.

3. Add the queen, drones and workers.

4. Add eggs, larvae and pupae.

5. Show off your model or drawing to another person. Explain what social insects are, and a little about each of their different jobs.

Chapter 4

Finding and Collecting Insects

Finding and Collecting Insects

FINDING INSECTS

You can learn a lot about insects by watching live insects outdoors to see what they do.

To find them, look in fields and gardens and in woodsy places. Look in trees and bushes, on the ground, under grass and leaves, and under logs and rocks.

Flying insects can be found near flowers and trees in the daytime. At night many insects can be found near an outdoor light—the light attracts them.

COLLECTING INSECTS

To see insects up close, you can catch them. To do this you will need a collecting jar.

If you don't want to kill the insects, punch holes in the lid of the jar with a hammer and a nail to let air in. Put some soil and leaves and grass in the jar. Catch the insect, and put the lid on.

You can catch crawling insects by having them crawl on a piece of paper, then shaking them into your jar.

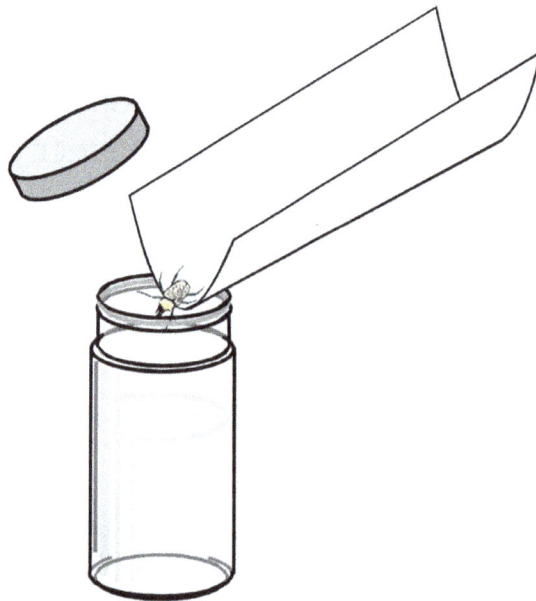

For collecting flying insects you will need a net. The net should be round and have a handle on it. The net part should be quite a bit

longer than the width at the hoop. Then you can turn the hoop to trap a butterfly in the bottom of the net.

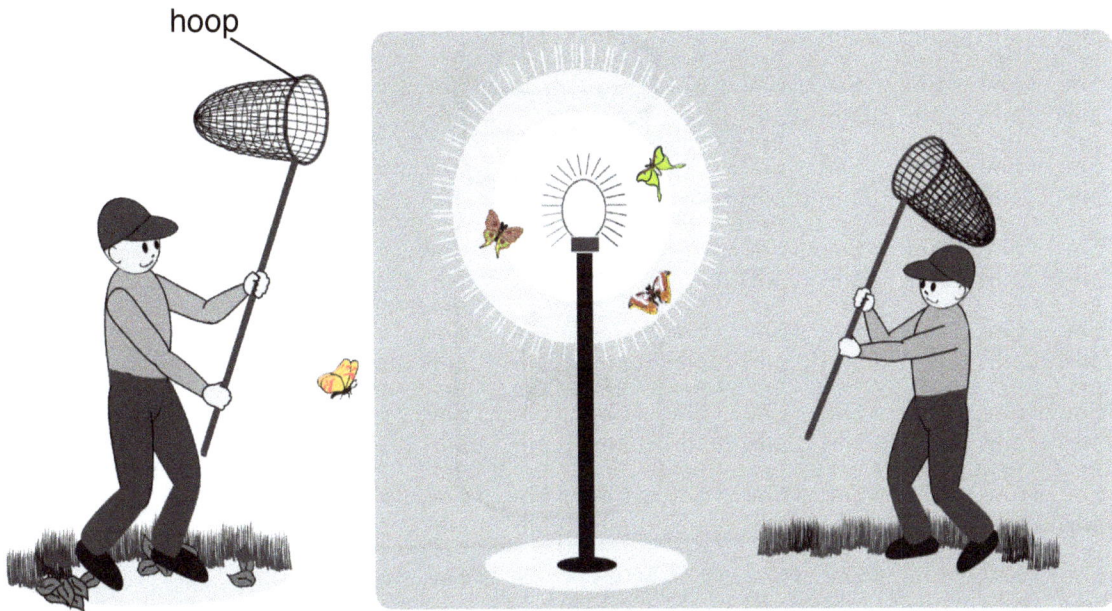

hoop

To see even better what insects look like, and to display them, you can kill some of them.

The first thing you will need is a killing jar. The killing jar is a jar with rubbing alcohol in it. Rubbing alcohol is a special, clear liquid that can be used to kill insects and keep them from rotting.

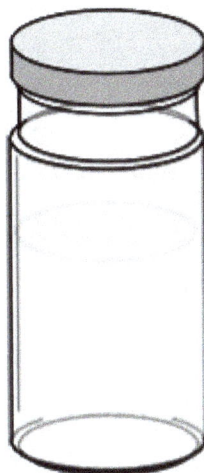

When you have caught an insect, you put it into the jar of alcohol and close the top.

The insect will soon die.

When the insect is dead, take it out of the alcohol and pin it in a display box with a pin through the insect's back. This is called **mounting** the insect.

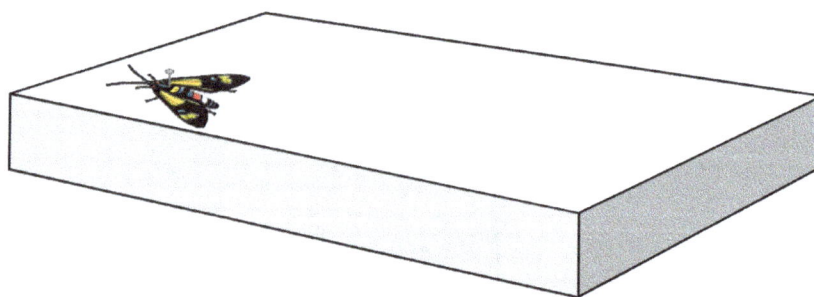

display box

If the insect is too small to stick a pin through, glue it to a small piece of paper, and pin the paper.

Write a letter by each insect you pin in your box. Then write that letter on another piece of paper and next to it write what kind of insect it is (if you know) and where you found it.

So your display box would look something like this:

INSECTS

A. Housefly
Found in my house

B. Ladybug
Found on a flower

C. Butterfly
Found in a tree

You can learn many things about insects by catching them, mounting them, and looking at them very closely.

Chapter 5

So Many Insects!

Chapter 5

So Many Insects!

There are so many different kinds of insects that it would be impossible to count them all. In fact, there are more different kinds of insects than all other kinds of animals combined! There are over 700,000 different kinds of insects in the world, and more than 88,000 just in North America.

Here are just a few of the many, many different kinds of insects.

ANTS

There are a lot of different kinds of ants. They can be different shapes and sizes, and they can be gray, brown, black or red. They live nearly everywhere in the world.

We already know a lot about ants, such as that they are social insects. Here is a little more interesting information about them.

The queens and the males have wings when they are mating. The workers don't have wings at all.

After she has mated, the queen goes into the nest to stay. She starts laying eggs, and that will be her job for the rest of her life. She tears off her wings because she will never need to fly again.

Ants eat many things including leaves, dead plants and animals, and nectar from flowers.

APHIDS

Aphids (A-fids) are small insects that suck the sap from plant leaves, stems and roots. When they eat, they release a clear sweet liquid called *honeydew*.

Ants and other insects eat the honeydew made by aphids. Some ants carry aphids from plant to plant, making sure the aphids have enough to eat so the ants can have plenty of honeydew. Some ants even keep aphid eggs in their ant colony over the winter so they can be sure of having honeydew again in the spring. You could say that these ants are "aphid farmers!"

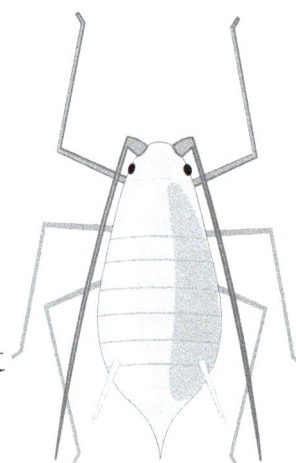

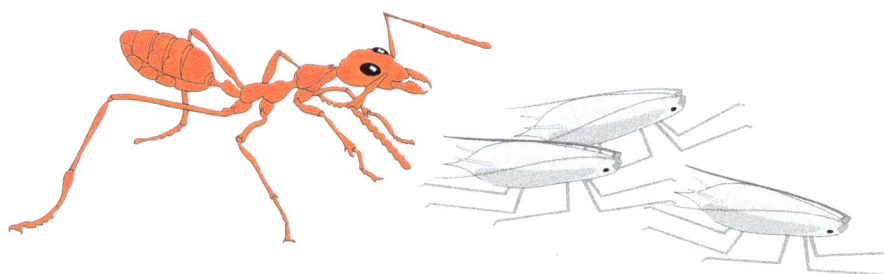

Ants would not agree, but humans think aphids are pests. A **pest** is an animal that does something annoying or harmful. The reason humans think aphids are pests is because they injure farm and garden crops or house plants. They are so small you might not see that they were there before they did some damage.

Aphids can also be annoying in the city. If you park a car under a tree where aphids are eating, you might come out later to find it covered with tiny drops of sticky honeydew.

CICADAS

Cicadas (si-CAY-duz) are insects that are related to aphids but are much bigger. Cicadas also eat plant parts. Cicada nymphs eat the roots of trees, and adult cicadas eat the leaves.

Adult cicadas lay eggs on twigs. After the eggs hatch, the nymphs drop to the ground. They crawl into the ground and start feeding on the sap of the roots.

Cicada nymphs live in the ground for a long time, usually several years, eating and molting and growing, before they crawl up the tree to molt one last time and become adults.

When they come out of the ground, they are called a **swarm**. There can be trillions of cicadas in a swarm!

Adult male cicadas are noisy. They make a humming or buzzing sound. When they all buzz at once it can be very loud. For five or six weeks, they make their sounds to find their mates. The females lay their eggs on the trees, and then all the adults die, and it starts all over again.

Certain cicada nymphs stay in the ground for 17 years! These cicadas are also called "seventeen-year locusts." (They are not actually locusts—true locusts are a kind of grasshopper.) A year that a lot of these cicadas come out of the ground and start eating the leaves off of trees and buzzing all day long is often remembered as "the year of the locusts" by the people who live in the area.

TERMITES

Termites are social insects that live in the ground and in wood. They look similar to ants but they are not true ants. Termites are usually pale tan colored or tan striped with brown.

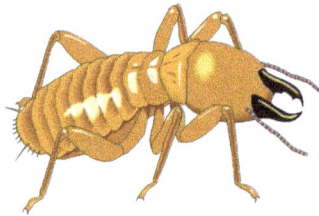

Most termites eat dead wood. Some eat the wood of live trees.

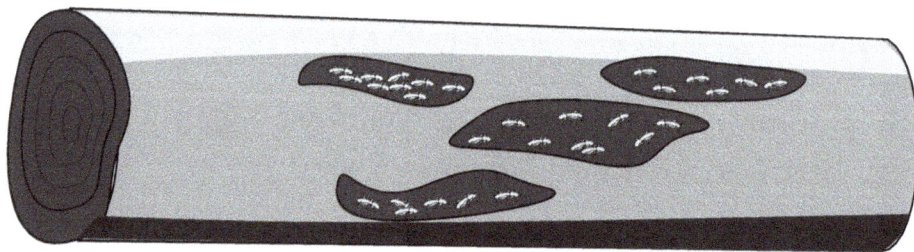

There are four kinds of termites in a termite colony: the king, the queen, the workers and the soldiers.

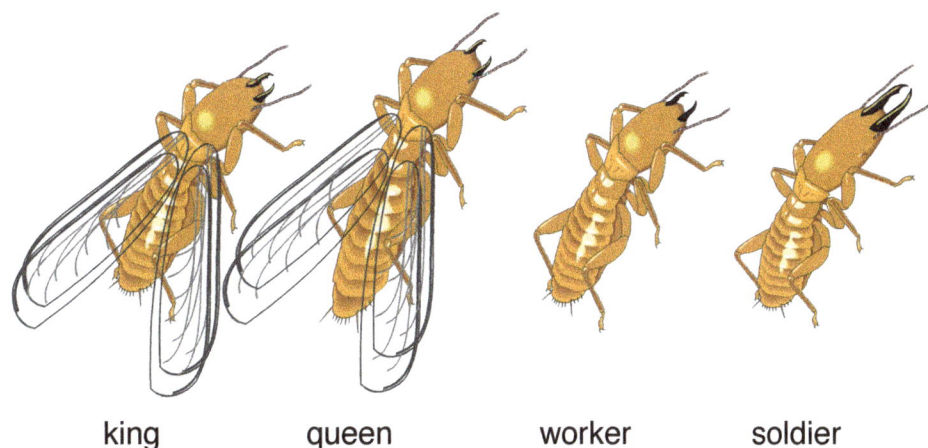

king   queen   worker   soldier

The king and queen are the only ones that have wings. The queen lays eggs. The king's job is to mate with the queen.

The worker termites build the colony by digging holes in wood, and they gather food.

The soldiers protect the colony from enemies such as ants. The soldiers have big claws on their heads to fight with.

The only time termites have wings is when a colony gets big enough that it needs to start a new colony. This happens when a colony is about three to four years old. Then termites with wings hatch, and they fly off to start a new colony.

Some termites are good because they help get rid of old dead wood in forests. Some termites are pests because they eat the wood of fences and houses, which can weaken these things and make them collapse.

BEETLES

There are more kinds of beetles than any other insect—thousands and thousands of different kinds. They make up more than a third of all the insects in the world. Beetles come in all shapes and sizes, but they all have hard front wings that fold to cover their back wings. The two front wings come together to make a straight line down their backs.

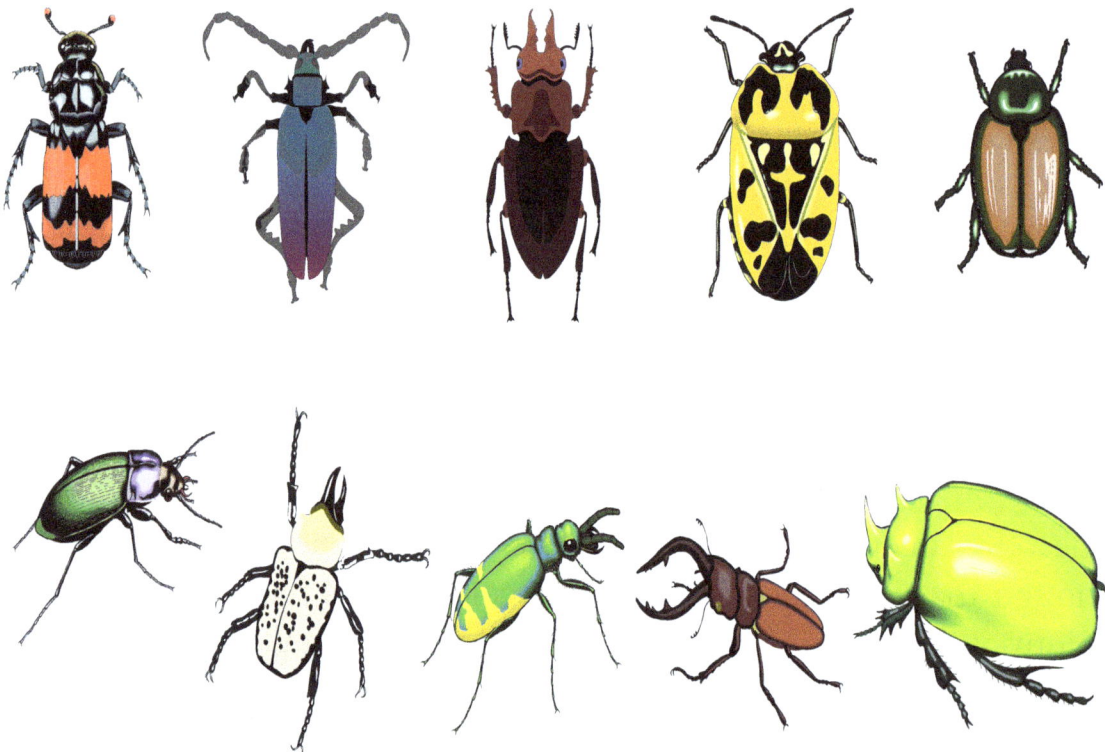

Beetles raise these hard covers and use just their back wings to fly.

Different beetles eat different kinds of food. No matter what kind of food you can think of, there is probably a kind of beetle somewhere that would eat it. For example, dung beetles eat dung (another word for poop!). One kind of dung beetle rolls it into round balls, and buries it to eat later or use it as a place to lay their eggs.

Ladybugs are sometimes called ladybird beetles. They are small round beetles, red or orange colored with dark spots on their backs.

Ladybugs have wings and can fly, but they crawl most of the time. They are not afraid of people and will crawl on your fingers if you let them. Some people think it is lucky to have a flying ladybug land on them.

Ladybugs are helpful to humans because they eat other insects that harm crops and gardens, like aphids. Sometimes farmers buy thousands of ladybugs in boxes and release them in fields to help get rid of other insect pests.

GRASSHOPPERS AND CRICKETS

Grasshoppers and crickets are hopping insects. They are usually about one inch long, but in some parts of the world they can grow to be as much as six inches long! They have big strong back legs that make them able to jump a long way. Grasshoppers are usually green, brown or gray. Crickets are usually darker in color.

grasshopper

cricket

Grasshoppers and crickets eat leaves and other parts of plants. There are many kinds of crickets and grasshoppers. One kind of hump-backed grasshopper is called the katydid.

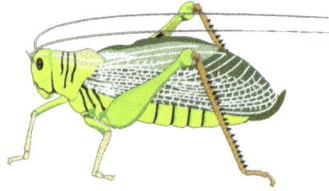

Most crickets don't fly at all, and grasshoppers don't fly much, but one kind of grasshopper, often called locusts, fly together in big swarms from field to field and can do much damage to crops by eating them. However, most grasshoppers and crickets are helpful to humans because they eat weeds.

Some grasshoppers, crickets and katydids make buzzing, singing or chirping sounds by rubbing their wings or legs together. You often may hear these sounds during warm, sunny days. The warmer it gets, the more often a cricket will chirp.

Mantises, walking sticks and cockroaches (often just called "roaches") are all related to the grasshopper and cricket families.

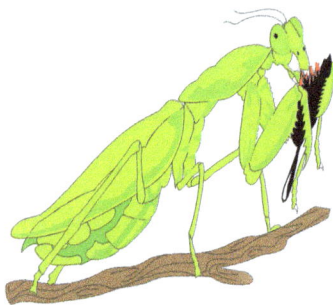

mantis   cockroach   walking stick

As you can see, mantises and walking sticks are particularly odd looking. The mantis uses its strong front legs to catch and hold the insects it eats. When a walking stick isn't walking, it is hard to tell it from a real stick.

Cockroaches are a pest to humans, because they like to live in people's homes to go after their food, and they are hard to get rid of. They are one of the oldest groups of insects. They have been around hundreds of millions of years!

FLEAS

Fleas are small black insects without wings.

Fleas live in the fur of animals and in the feathers of birds. Fleas bite the skin of the animal and suck out some blood.

Fleas like to live on dogs and cats. Flea bites itch, so if a dog or cat scratches a lot, it probably has fleas on it.

Fleas can jump farther than a foot. Sometimes they jump onto people and bite them. Fleas are pests to people and animals.

FLIES

There are about 125,000 kinds of flies in the world. The way you can tell if a flying insect is actually a fly is by their wings. They have only one pair of wings.

Other insects that have wings have two pairs—a front pair and a back pair.

Two kinds of flies that you are probably very familiar with are houseflies and mosquitoes.

HOUSEFLIES

Houseflies and their larvae (called *maggots*) eat dead plants and animals, garbage and household food.

Houseflies cannot bite, but they can carry harmful germs on their bodies and can spread diseases if they land on food. They have a bad habit of spitting up some of the last food they ate onto the next food they land on. Food for people should be kept away from flies.

MOSQUITOES

Mosquitoes have tube-like mouth parts for sucking their food. You may not know that it's only female mosquitoes that suck blood from animals and people. Male mosquitoes eat by sucking the juices out of plants.

When a mosquito bites someone, some of its saliva (spit) goes into the skin. The saliva keeps the blood thin enough to suck. It also makes an itchy bump.

Mosquitoes can spread diseases among animals and people. If a mosquito bites a sick person and then bites a well person, some disease germs from the sick person's blood may get into the well person's body.

The larvae of mosquitoes live in water and are sometimes called "wrigglers" because of the way they move. They hang just under the surface of the water and breathe through air tubes at the end of their abdomen. If it rains during the summer and some puddles stay for a few days, you may find wigglers in the puddles. These wigglers will change into mosquitoes soon. But you can kill them by putting a little oil on the puddle. This will keep them from being able to breathe.

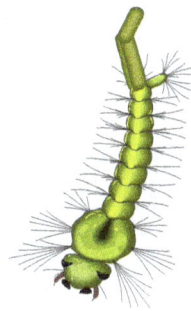

Mosquitoes are pest insects that are found nearly everywhere in the world.

BUTTERFLIES AND MOTHS

There are many, many different kinds of butterflies. Their bright wings can have many different designs and colors.

Butterflies usually fold their wings straight up and tight together when they are not flying.

Adult butterflies suck the juice from flowers and help the flowers get ready to make seeds by spreading pollen. Pollen is the yellow dust on flowers.

The larvae of butterflies are caterpillars. Caterpillars eat leaves and can be a pest because they eat plants from farms and gardens.

Moths look very much like butterflies. Their wings are the same shape as butterflies' wings. But moths hold their wings out flat to the sides of their bodies when they land. Also their bodies are fatter and rounder, and their feelers are different from those of butterflies. Their feelers often look a bit like feathers.

Moths also come in many different colors. There are many different types of moths.

Moths only come out at night. You hardly ever see them flying during the day. Moths are attracted to light at night, but hide in the daytime. You can often see them around a light at night.

The larvae of moths are caterpillars, and look much like the larvae of butterflies. They eat mostly the leaves of plants and trees. Some of these caterpillars can be quite destructive to trees.

Some adult moths lay their eggs in clothing or carpets, and when the eggs hatch, the moth larvae will eat the cloth. These are called clothes moths or carpet moths, and are pests to people.

One helpful kind of moth called the silkworm moth spins its cocoon out of silk threads. People collect the cocoons and use the threads to make a fine, smooth cloth called silk.

BEES AND WASPS

Bees and wasps are flying insects that are closely related to ants. There are many different kinds of bees and wasps. Some kinds of bees and wasps are social insects that make nests or hives, but others live alone.

Bees are generally yellow and brown and have tiny hairs covering their bodies. Wasps are usually darker in color and do not have as much fuzzy hair.

bumblebee   honeybee   wasp

Some bees and wasps eat the bodies of dead animals.

Other kinds eat the nectar and pollen from flowers and tree blossoms. Like butterflies, these kinds also help flowers make seeds by carrying pollen that sticks to their feet from flower to flower.

Honeybees are a type of social bee that people raise to get the honey they make. Honeybees make wax honeycombs with little holes to store their honey in.

After they fill the holes, they cover them with more wax.

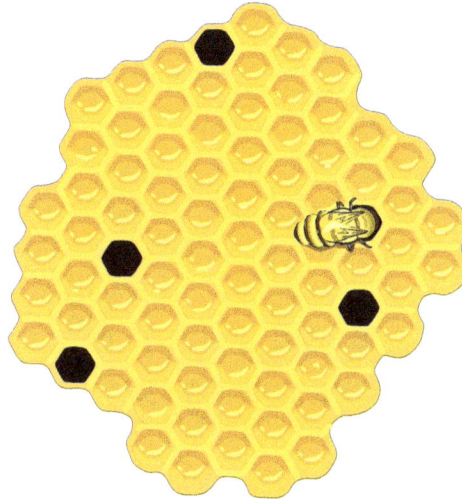

People can take the honey and the wax from the honeycombs to use. The honey is sweet to eat, and the wax is used for making candles and other things.

SO MANY INSECTS!

These are just a tiny few of all of the insects of the world. There is so much to know about them that there are special scientists who just study insects. Their jobs are discovering more and more about these fascinating creatures that are all around us.

LET'S DO THIS!
Find Out More

For this activity you will need

- access to internet

Steps

1. Choose an insect you want to learn more about.

2. Have an adult help you find a short online video or article for children about the insects you choose.

3. Here are some questions you could find out answers to. Pick one or two, or think of your own questions.

    - What do they look like?
    - Are they social insects or not?
    - Do they do a complete or incomplete metamorphosis?
    - What do they look like in the different parts of their metamorphosis?
    - What do they eat?
    - What eats them?
    - Are they pests to humans or are they helpful?

4. Write down the answers to the questions, and anything else interesting you learned.

5. Draw at least one picture of something you learned.

6. Tell (or write-up for) another person what you find out, and show off your drawing.

Chapter 6

Living with Insects

Chapter 6

Living with Insects

There are more insects in the world than all other animals put together. If you could pack all the insect bodies together in one lump, and do the same with all other animals combined, the insects would make a bigger lump!

Insects live mostly on land. Some kinds live on or in fresh water for at least part of their lives, and a very few live in the oceans. But on land they can be found almost everywhere.

Most insects have wings and can fly. This gives them a big advantage when they need to escape from another animal. You know that this is true if you have ever tried to swat a pesky fly.

Even though there are so many insects, we do not often see most of them because they are very small and they hide well.

Even though insects are small, they can affect humans in big ways. Some insects are harmful because they eat the crops in fields and gardens. And some insects are very good and useful to have around.

HARMFUL

Locusts are one kind of insect that can be harmful. Locusts are a type of grasshopper, and they eat all kinds of plants. They sometimes swarm in big groups. When there are many of them, they can destroy whole fields of crops in a short time.

Termites are insects that eat wood. They help get rid of dead trees in the forests, which is very good. But if they get into the wood of houses, they can weaken or destroy them.

Clothes moths can eat and ruin people's clothes if they get into their closets.

Weevils are insects that eat grain and cotton plants. If they get into people's crops, they can destroy them. They can also get into grain and flour in people's kitchens.

Grubs are beetle larvae that live in the ground and eat the roots of plants. They can damage lawns and gardens.

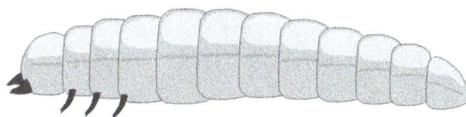

Other insects, such as mosquitoes, lice and fleas, live by getting on animals and sucking blood from them. When they bite or sting people they can cause an itching or hurting bump.

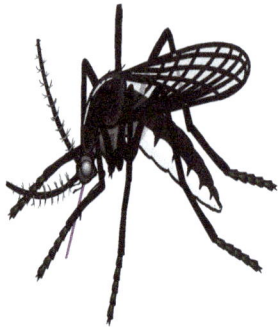

mosquito   louse (plural "lice")   flea

These biting insects may also spread disease. They do this by first biting a sick person and then later biting another person and giving the sickness to that person.

Sometimes people try to poison insect pests and kill them so they cannot do harm. Sometimes this is very helpful but it is not always a good idea, because the poison may kill good insects as well as the bad ones.

HELPFUL

Only a few of the many kinds of insects are truly harmful to people. Most are important to the world.

One of the most important things insects do is help plants make new seeds. Insects go from flower to flower and carry some of the pollen with them. Moving the pollen from flower to flower helps the flowers be able to make seeds that will become new plants.

Many kinds of trees and plants could not make new trees and plants if it were not for insects helping them.

Insects also help make the soil better for new plants to grow in. Insects eat dead plants and animals (including dead insects) on the ground and turn them into materials that make the soil better.

Another way insects are helpful is that they are food for many, many different birds, fish, reptiles, amphibians and mammals. If not for insects, many of the animals that people eat for food would not exist!

Some insects catch and eat other insects. Insects that eat other insects are helpful to people because they help keep the number of other insects from getting too large.

Some insects are helpful in special ways. We already know how honeybees give us honey and beeswax.

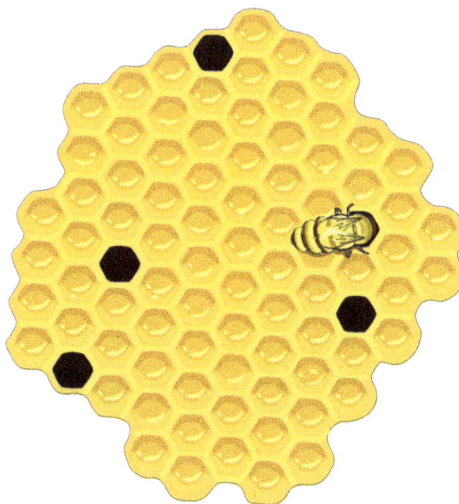

And we know about the silkworm moth larva that spins threads of silk when it is making its cocoon. People collect the cocoons and unwind them, and use the threads to make beautiful silk clothes. Up to a thousand yards of silk can be unwound from just one cocoon!

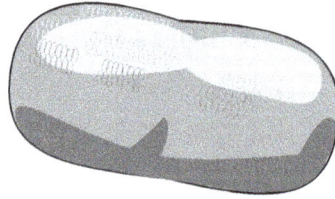

Insects are a very important part of the world, and affect other animals and plants in many, many ways. Now you know a few of those ways!

LET'S DO THIS!
Find Insects Outdoors

For this activity you will need

- magnifying glass
- collecting jar (jar with soil, leaves and grass, and lid with holes punched in it)
- notebook
- net for collecting flying insects, if available

Steps

1. With a magnifying glass, notebook, collecting jar, and net if you have one, go outdoors and look for flying and crawling insects, larvae and pupae.

2. Using the magnifying glass if possible, for any insect you find observe at least these things:

   - their hard covering,
   - their three main body parts,
   - where their legs and wings are attached, and how they move.

3. Using the magnifying glass, observe any larvae and pupae you find. Notice how they are different from adult insects.

4. Take notes on what you observe, and draw any pictures you wish to.

5. Collect several of the insects, larvae and pupae you find.

6. Here are some suggestions for finding insects:

   - If it is spring, summer or fall, try looking for a ladybug. Look in trees and bushes.

   - If it is summer and the sun is out, go into a grassy area away from people and buildings and listen for a high buzzing sound. If you hear it, see if you can find the grasshopper or cricket that is making that sound.

   - Look for larvae in trees, in the grass, under rocks and on the ground.

   - Look for pupae in trees, on branches and on leaves. Pupae are usually in round shells.

7. Come back inside with the insects you collected.

8. If you don't already know, have someone help you see if you can find out what kind of insects you have collected by looking online or in an insect book.

9. Make a drawing of each of the insects, label each insect as well as you can, and write a little about where you found it, and anything else you noticed about it.

10. Show your jar and your drawing to another person. Explain how you know these are insects, and answer any questions.

11. Go outside and let your insects out.

LET'S DO THIS!
More Activities with Insects

STUDY ALL THE INSECTS ON A PATCH OF GROUND

For this activity you will need

- notebook
- magnifying glass

Steps

1. Go outside to a nearby wooded area and mark off a square on the ground about one foot on each side.

2. Gently pick any loose leaves and grass off the soil in this area so you can see what insects are there.

3. Using the magnifying glass to look closely at any insect you find, observe at least these things:

   - their hard covering,
   - their three main body parts
   - where their legs and wings are attached, and how they move.

4. Using the magnifying glass, observe any larvae you find. Notice how they are different from adult insects.

5. If you don't see enough insects, move your square to a different place.

6. For each insect you find, note down what step of life it is in. If you know what kind of insect it is, write down its name. If you can't tell what it is, make a picture of it so you can look it up later. Also decide if you think it is a helpful insect or a pest.

7. Keep doing this until you have found at least ten different kinds of insects.

8. Make a list of all the insects you found. (For any you don't already know, have someone help you see if you can find out what kind of insects you have collected by looking online or in an insect book.)

9. Draw a picture of your favorite insect.

10. Show another person your list and drawing. Explain how you know these are insects, and answer any questions.

RAISE ANTS IN AN ANT FARM

For this activity you will need

- ant farm kit (available from Amazon)

Steps

1. An ant farm is some dirt or sand closed between two pieces of glass or clear plastic like a sandwich. You put ants in it and some food for them and watch how they make tunnels and nests to live in. Most ant farms you can buy don't provide queens, just workers.

2. Once you have your ant farm kit, set it up according to the instructions.

3. Take care of your ant farm every day by making sure the ants have food and water.

4. Watch your ant farm every day and see what your ants are doing. Count how many different jobs there are to do in the colony.

5. If it is good weather, go outside and look for ant colonies. If you find one, watch it closely. Watch a worker ant bring food back to the colony. You could also drop a small crumb near the colony. See how long it takes for the ants to discover it.

6. When enough days have gone by for you to have seen the ants doing different jobs, show your ant farm to another person and explain what ant workers are, and all the different jobs you saw the workers do.

CATCH SOME BUTTERFLIES AND MOTHS

For this activity you will need

- insect net
- notebook
- drawing materials
- collection jar

Steps

1. If it is spring, summer or fall, go outside with an insect net and notebook and find some butterflies.

2. Watch them for a while before you catch them, and make notes about where and when you found them and what they were doing.

3. Catch one or two, put them in a jar and look at them closely. Observe at least these things:

   - their hard covering,
   - their three main body parts
   - where their legs and wings are attached, and how they move.

4. Try to find a caterpillar and put it in a jar. Compare how they look. Remember they are different steps in the life of the same insect.

5. Draw a picture of your butterflies to show the colors and patterns on their wings.

6. Let your butterflies go.

7. Go outside with your net at night and find some moths.

8. Watch them for a while before you catch them, and make notes about where and when you found them and what they were doing.

9. Catch one or two, put them in a jar and look at them closely. Observe at least these things:

   - their hard covering,
   - their three main body parts
   - where their legs and wings are attached, and how they move.

10. Draw a picture of your moths to show the colors and patterns on their wings.

11. Let your moths go.

12. Show another person your drawings. Explain what you did for this activity, what you observed, and the difference you noticed between the butterflies and the moths. Answer any questions.

MAKE AN INSECT DISPLAY

For this activity you will need

- insect net (if flying insects are wanted)
- killing jar (jar with alcohol in it and lid)
- display box with pins (can be a piece of cardboard)

Steps

1. Catch at least ten different kinds of insects that you would like to display, and kill them with a killing jar. (See chapter 4.) You can use any insects you already caught for another project if you wish.

2. Mount your insects on a display box with pins. (chapter 4.)

3. Write down for each insect where and when you found it and what kind it is.

4. Show off your display box to another person. Tell the person the different things that make each an insect, and point these out. Answer any questions.

STUDY WILD BEES

For this activity you will need

- drawing materials

Steps

1. If it is spring or summer, go outside to where there are some flowers and see if you can find bees.

2. Watch them carefully and see what they do on the flowers. See how they go from flower to flower. (Don't swat them or try to catch them or they might sting you.)

3. You can try to follow a bee until it goes back to its beehive. If you find a hive, watch the bees going in and out and notice how many there are. Notice if they go to all the flowers or if they pick a certain kind. Notice how far the bees go away from their hive to collect the nectar from flowers. (If you do this, you might be in for quite a hike. Bees may go a mile or more away from their hive.)

4. Draw a picture of one of the bees you saw, showing what it was doing on the flower.

5. Show your drawing to another person, and explain how you know that bees are insects.

STUDY BEES AT A BEE FARM

For this activity you will need

- access to a bee farm or any place that keeps bees
- drawing materials

Steps

1. Go to a place where they keep bees for honey.

2. See if someone there will give you a tour and tell you about it. Possibly someone can even show you the inside of a hive.

3. Find out what kinds of bees are raised there. Find out what the bees eat, and how long it takes for them to fill the beehives with honey.

4. Watch the bees closely, and draw pictures of them and a hive.

5. Show your drawings to another person, and explain what you learned about keeping bees.

STUDY DARKLING BEETLE METAMORPHOSIS

For this activity you will need

- access to the internet
- drawing materials

Steps

1. Find a picture online of a mealworm or darkling beetle life cycle. (Mealworm is what the larva of a darkling beetle is called.)

2. Find a video online of a darkling beetle or mealworm metamorphosis, and watch it. Notice the different parts of its metamorphosis. Is it a complete metamorphosis or an incomplete metamorphosis?

3. Draw a picture of this insect at each part of its life. When you are done, you should have a drawing of a larva, a pupa, an adult insect and insect eggs. Label your drawing.

4. Show your drawing to another person, and explain what a complete metamorphosis is and also what an incomplete metamorphosis is.

STUDY INSECTS AT A MUSEUM

For this activity you will need

- access to a science museum that has a display about insects
- drawing materials

Steps

1. Go to a science museum and look at all the displays about insects.

2. Pick your favorite display and draw a picture of it. Learn all you can from the display about the insects you picked.

3. If this was not a big display with more than one type of insect in it, find another one you like and draw a picture of it too.

4. Keep doing this until you have learned all about five different insects.

5. Show another person all your drawings, and explain what you learned about the insects.

WATCH A VIDEO ABOUT INSECTS

For this activity you will need

- access to internet
- globe or map

Steps

1. Have an adult help you find a short online video or article for children about insects that you want to learn more about. You might get a video on insects that eat other insects, or one about insect metamorphosis.

2. Watch the video, and notice things you have learned about insects, like what makes them insects, the different parts of their lives, and so on.

3. Look at a globe or map to find the place where the insects in the video live.

4. Decide what parts of the video you liked best, and draw pictures to show what happened in that part.

5. Show your drawings to another person, and explain what you have learned about insects that you noticed in the video.

DO YOUR OWN SPECIAL INSECTS PROJECT

Steps

1. Think of a project about insects that you can do that isn't on this list. For example, maybe you know someone who studies insects and takes pictures of them, and you can learn about that.

2. Tell another person what you want to do, and how you will do it.

3. Do your project.

4. Tell another person everything you did and what you learned.